THE REAL CAUSE FOR YOUR ABSENCE

poems

Curtis Bauer

THE REAL CAUSE FOR YOUR ABSENCE

All Rights Reserved.

Second Edition

2 3 4 5 6 7 8 9 10

No more than four lines of any one portion of this book may be reproduced or used in any form or reproduced by any means without written permission from publishers John Gosslee and Andrew Sullivan.

Copyright © 2013 by Curtis Bauer

ISBN: 9781936196234
LCCN: 2012945755

Cover image LA Parking Lot by Bronlyn Jones

Author photo by Idoia Elola

Cover and book design by Angela Plagmann
plagmanngraphics.com

C&R Press
Conscious & Responsible
crpress.org

ACKNOWLEDGMENTS

The author wishes to thank the editors of the publications in which the following poems appeared, though sometimes in a different incarnation and under a different title: *32 Poems*: Experienced Worker, Employment Wanted; *Barrow Street*: Aviary; *The American Poetry Review*: Seeing A Tan Woman's Face, Late Winter; *Asheville Poetry Review*: Three Spain Sketches; *CUTTHROAT, A Journal of the Arts*: Whiteout; *Diagram*: Still Life With A Bed In The Middle; *Folio*: The Immaculate Heart; In A Northern Province; *Fugue*: Beginning with a Eucalyptus Leaf; *Fulcrum*: El Ejido; While Hydrangeas Are Falling; Letter From A Foreign Country; Six This Morning; Sketchbook Sonnets #53 & #54—A Dust Speck That Used To Be A Man; The Tornadoes In You; *GSU Review*: Still Life With A Man Falling Through It; *The Indiana Review*: Colony Collapse Disorder; *The Iron Horse Literary Review*: The Fall; I Open A Beer, A Car Approaches; *Main Street Rag*: Following Instructions; *Ninth Letter*: Matins; Passages North: You Know You Want It; *Rivendell*: Recital; *Runes*: Becoming A Crow; *Salamander*: Home; *Spillway*: Drawing Of A Woman's Silence; *The Tampa Review*: Jacaranda Love Song; *Tar River Poetry*: Looking At 12 White Things

The poem "Whiteout" was selected by Marvin Bell as the runner-up for the 2010 Joy Harjo Poetry Contest, sponsored by *CUTTHROAT, A Journal of the Arts*. The poem "Experienced Worker, Employment Wanted" appears in the anthology *Poetry Doesn't Need You: From the First 10 years of 32 Poems Magazine*. The poems, in English and Spanish translation, "Three Spain Sketches," "Jacaranda Love Song," "Recital," "El Ejido," "While Hydrangeas Are Falling," "Letter From A Foreign Country," "Six This Morning," "In A Northern Province," "Beginning with a Eucalyptus Leaf," "Still Life With A Bed In The Middle," "Valle de Atxondo," "While Reading I Think About Drawing," "Lilac In Sevilla," "Saetas," "To the Birds Outside My Window," and "If This Is What It Takes" appeared in the bilingual collection *Spanish Sketchbook/España en dibujos* (Ediciones en Huida, Seville, Spain, 2012).

I am grateful to more people than I can thank here for their kindness, friendship and critical wisdom during the writing of this book, though especially I want to thank Kurt Caswell, Karen Clark, Hafid Gafaiti, John Poch, Adam Houle, Ryan Walsh, Elaine Sexton, Jennifer Acker, Jackie Brookner, Brad Holst, as well as my friends and colleagues at From the Fishouse, my students and colleagues at Texas Tech, and my mentors, whose voices I carry with me, always. I also want to thank the Vermont Studio Center and the Resedencía Elola-Astiazaran in Atxondo for their space and kindness, where many of these poems found their form.

Special thanks to my family—Ross Gay for his blooming criticism, his joy and patience, to Patrick Rosal for picking up the phone, teaching me music, dance and reminding me of what I need to know, to Alex Long and Sebastian Matthews for helping this book take shape and for their relentless generosity, and Angela Plagmann for her invaluable creative input and patience.

And to Idoia, the beautiful, brilliant Basque who has taken my hands in hers—all my love.

For Sebastian, dear friend and brother

e Idoia, por supuesto

CONTENTS

If This Is What It Takes   7

ONE

Experienced Worker, Employment Wanted   10
The Tornadoes In You   11
You Know You Want It!   12
Seeing A Tan Woman's Face, Late Winter   13
To A Woman Standing In A Doorway
     Watching The Rain   14
Looking On The Yard Wednesday Morning   16
Acceleration   17
Becoming A Crow   18
Walking By   24
Matins   25
Drawing Of A Woman's Silence   26
The Real Cause For Your Absence   28
A History Of Oak Trees   29
Aviary   30
Still Life With A Bed In The Middle   31
Looking At 12 White Things   32
Still Life With A Man Falling Through It   33
Postcard   35
A Place Like This   36
The Fall   37
Following Instructions   39
I Open A Beer, A Car Approaches   40

TWO

Six This Morning   42
Rant   43
Colony Collapse Disorder   44
Recital   47
Reading Richard Hugo To My Niece   48
Walking Around   50

Drawing Of A Boy Forgetting 51
Lunch With The Kiwanis Club 53
Whiteout 54

THREE

Home 57
Three Spain Sketches 58
Letter From Another Country 61
Jacaranda Love Song 62
Sketchbook Sonnet #38—On Clouds 63
Beginning With A Eucalyptus Leaf 64
Sketchbook Sonnets #53 & #54—
      A Dust Speck That Used To Be A Man 65
South Overton 67
Sketchbook Sonnet #86—A Northern Province 69
While Hydrangeas Are Falling 70
Valle De Atxondo 71
While Reading I Think About Drawing 72
El Ejido 73
Saetas 74
Lilac In Sevilla 75
Drawings 76

Notes 78

We keep coming back and coming back
To the real: to the hotel instead of the hymns
That fall upon it out of the wind.

   —WALLACE STEVENS

IF THIS IS WHAT IT TAKES

The knife in your hand wants flesh—

its appetite for blood is sharp steel

leaning, weeping into the tomato's meat,

sugar beets, steaming rhubarb pie—and hunts

that juice etching your hands, pulsing

your neck and shifting your hips. You

slice, you bleed, you leak into pools bubbling

the countertop, over the scuffed linoleum

to the stainless steel sink and anoint the potato

peelings, onion skins and apple rinds.

Make your salad before rot sets in

and that side of you that turns my head

after we've parted on the street

to watch your steps escapes. You come to me

squeezing your bleeding as if it were a gift,

as if the more you bled the better you'd feel

offering your invitation to join the thin red

sliver seething and throbbing your hands

into mine. Beautiful bleeder, my hands

never held holy powers until they entangled yours.

A blade, I understand its language. Give me

the knife and press its edge here. Pull.

ONE

If you don't want to stay and watch the storm
I will watch it for you.

—JUAN ANTONIO GONZÁLEZ IGLESIAS

EXPERIENCED WORKER, EMPLOYMENT WANTED

I watch the dead gather on the sidewalks
from my car. Every Friday I remind
the garbage man of his promises. I talk

to the old women stranded on the street
corners, pick up their teeth when they fall
from their mouths; I know how to wait

for traffic to thin, for the Dutch bakers
to throw out their scraps and the butcher
to kill a hog. I should add that I am multi-

lingual and the translator of last squeals:
in this instance it means the pig is confused.
I understand pigs; they don't like confusion.

I dig back yard crypts, line them with pine
paneling and shelves; I stock them with wine
and fine cheeses. I'd like to add spoons,

guitars and cellos, but music sounds off
when it's tarnished and warped. Still, I will
teach myself to play these instruments.

I am not honest. I bake stale bread for the starving
swallows shivering in the cold air. They are nervous
little birds, always afraid. I know their history:

a man threw a torch down the chimney of their temple
because he wanted to see fire fly. It flew as it burned
an arc in the tails of swallows small enough to fit

in the palm of his hand. Their song repeats,
repeats this memory—they keen for their brothers
and sisters when pecking crumbs from my palm.

THE TORNADOES IN YOU

This woman I love says, *Let's play
tornadoes*,

and tells me she once thought all wind was born
and died in her lungs.

Today
she knows

those were a child's needs to understand
the secrets of afternoons

and rain storms—this
blowing she loves, she knows,

never dies but keeps circling and pulling
in volcanic urges of air,

for example, from her hand on my neck
flurrying our clothes and rumpling the sheets,

the room atilt in atmospheric disruption,
a national disaster she reports

in a deep breath bracing
herself for another storm.

YOU KNOW YOU WANT IT!

a girl shouted
         at me and my friends
as we reeled out of our previous night's drunk.

How did she know I *did* want *it*, and all the word's
simplicity in her child's voice directing us
to her stand, to the green and orange

boxes of peanut butter and mint cookies,
the money I uncrumpled to buy those boxes
and the coffee we'd dip them in after juice

and eggs down the street, and what that cash
couldn't touch, like the soprano lilt
rising out of that immensely bruised

BBQ man on the south side singing in the rain,
and the woman behind him in the Velvet Lounge,
or if not all of her just another glance of her hand

on mine when I bought my gin, or
that smoked out feeling that's as close to bliss
as I've ever come walking down derelict city streets

without a car lights' glisten in a bawling storm?
Who thinks of faith waiting for the last train
among men who'd worked the hours before

while saxophone bleats and blabbers bounced
off glass? I should have. It was on their faces,
curled tight in their calloused hands, pulsing

in their paused scuffling home to a woman,
a man, a child, or an empty apartment's dry
bed before the sun. And I wanted it.

SEEING A TAN WOMAN'S FACE, LATE WINTER

It's January, New York, so she must be
back from somewhere nicer than here, but
sometimes I'll think about the big picture,
about my skin and perspective. I wonder
when I started to lie, when I began to trip
up and push all the verbs and nouns down
deep and flatten them out. I wonder where
green went, where joyous left tan and orange
and soft, smooth, yellowish coffee color
left my hand, and these blue eyes turned
their sight on some little grass blade and to
the mirror and my ruddy face. This morning
on my way to the airport, a woman on Lexington
with flowers, she's not just a woman, excuse me,
but she's not Sybil either because she wants to live
and she's beautiful and the flowers are white lilies
that make me think of spring, humming diesel engines
doing laps around fields and soil ready for planting,
ready for blooms, ready to germinate what touches it
and I want that *it* to be my hands, my eyes and why
do I have to think she looks like she can't afford those
cut flowers and now that I'm a thousand miles away
I see the flowers but not the hands, I can hear
the paper crinkle though I was in a car and speeding
and I want to hear her breath because it's even,
like the ambulance siren passing on the left
the taxi doesn't move over to let pass. The man
in the back is on a gurney and I hope he has
just had a long night at work and is tired,
so the sweat on his forehead and spittle
dribble at his mouth is natural and could be
a perfect reflection of me, right now seeing her.

TO A WOMAN STANDING IN A DOORWAY WATCHING THE RAIN

Rush out with me to where the lawns are wide,
where rain grows hands

that press the storm coming up behind us harder into your back
and my shoulders, and in the distance

light flashes green then yellow then red then green,
the traffic starts, speeds up,

stops, starts, quickens again before slowing down, stopping, waiting
under the sky above us piling upon

itself and pressing down because it can't go any higher, and the dark
forgets it should be dark and lets through

flashes, and then curses into the air—the rain falls harder, the light quicker,
the crackles, pings and booms faster

until oak, maple and willow leaves, paper cups, plastic bags, a crushed box,
everything and rain of course, all the liters

and gallons of rain fall
on us, cling to our ever heavier

steps, sodden shirts and sopping pants weighed down.
If you believe in the ineffable, dear

stranger, this is where our life can get interesting, like those stories in the books
a child scratches and smells for strawberries,

and geraniums as the pages leak colors and we realize slow and easy-like
we are witnesses of an impossible strength

for a moment, as it disobeys traffic laws, runs red lights, and slug-slow
divides in front of us a timeless frown, engulfs

the buildings and pushes the horizon forward, leaving us
standing at the light, drenched, uncertain

whether to keep walking together
or turn back alone.

LOOKING ON THE YARD WEDNESDAY MORNING

I'm back in this cluttered room reading
Zbigniew Herbert to the dark sky
and to the hoe I bought yesterday
at the hardware store when I needed
to buy a mailbox because someone
stole the basket we used for mail last
Sunday and left the dead sparrow while
we slept and woke speechless. That bird was
beautiful and almost smiling it
was so peaceful when I found it at
rest there on its side, as if it were
dreaming of flying with a big twig
twixt its feet. It grinned like I do now
using a word like *twixt* here, as if
it were flying with a huge twig. God,
I was filled with love for that bird, then
that love seeped away like water does
in search of lower ground, that place where
I buried the sparrow and broke two
twigs to mark its shallow, blessèd grave.

ACCELERATION

The street quiets.
The crows fly
north, the deepest part
of their black
commas and dashes above
the horizon,
and rush hour traffic
faded like a thought
no one put into words.
The crows leave
a dissipation of starlings,
cardinals, sparrows and mourning
doves, as if
they'd turned
a volume switch
off and quietly
accelerated past,
leaving behind bird song
and trees ignored
by passing hours,
a growing breeze
through the grass,
shifting the geranium pot
shadow shorter
and then longer.

BECOMING A CROW

The crows on the porch roof tap my window,
shout, laugh, list reasons to listen.

One nods at the man who curses the snow on his car.
Another at the mother angry with her child
for stopping to catch snow flakes on his tongue.

Another bobs his head: *Becoming darkness*, he says,
Letting the light bleed out of you is how you do this.

~

Today I'm trying to pull out my arms,
my toes and my ears. Inside me a crow
waits to emerge. I have gravel

in my throat. My feet shrivel and split,
raw bone tapping and clicking on the floor when I walk to the window.

I feel wings flap around me when I walk past my mother's house,
when I see a nibbled slice of pizza on the roadside.

I fly across the room and bounce off the wall.
I get strength from black corners,
from undersides of tables and bookshelves.

My eyes drain into my nose,
my teeth pull up to form my blue-black beak.

Arck, arck, arck, arck, arck, arck
I'm becoming a crow.

~

The murder waits
outside my window.
They are not laughing.

My arms have broken off at the elbow.
All the black nights I've walked,
consumed with my feet, seep
into my skin, turn my hair to opaque feathers.

~

I'm learning to squat and cackle
at the men on the street. This one
with the hat stares and smokes.

I'm learning to read the fear in his body.
My brothers tell me I was a fool,
but so is everyone else.
They watch the man on a ladder,
the jet trails,
the boy burning a doll with a match.

It's part of, they bark, *your nature.*

~

I thought these twigs would keep me awake,
but it's the laughter that bothers me the most.
I've heard this is the worst part for all of us.

~

In the morning I fly north
to chase the fence lines or follow
the rivers; I look for stones
and count grass blades. Dusk turns me
south. Tiny hands have tied failing light
to my tail feathers; all of us keep our beaks open
and fly. I am most comfortable then,
my wings touching the sky,
the growing dark massaging night
into it with each beat, like the ointment
my wife rubbed into my back
when I was a man. She is down there
on East Market, her eyes refusing to turn black,
her steps sifting the floor dust.
She paces from one room to the next,
holding her hands over her heart
to keep it from splitting again.

WALKING BY

A morning pulls from
the inside of night

the deep earth's moan,
the budging sound ground

makes when it slides. Call
it earth breath, or call

it rolling over,
or say *attrition*.

Maybe the ground thinks,

and a forgotten
well in the side yard

no one bothered to
fill speaks, and someone

carries blame for
why the dark spilled out

and tripped, then clung to
the man walking by.

MATINS

The factory whistle has blown. Open
the door and find unexpected heat and

a broken shoe lace bloated at the bottom
of a red puddle. Language is unidentifiable

color reflected in murky water, or a soul,
or the smell of dust and raspberries, diesel

fuel that seems carried here by the red-rumped
swallows coasting over a hill, birds in clouds

that make men stop their work, shush
the one who always has something to say

with their raised hands, so they can listen
in the middle of a landscape as dirt

clods crumble into dust, as clouds roll into another
morning when everything ordinary happens.

DRAWING OF A WOMAN'S SILENCE

Two nights after she stops speaking
my wife hums three bars in her sleep

as if she were thirty years older,
alone and washing clothes outside,

not as some kind of punishment
or indication of her line's poverty

even before the wars in her country,
and though hunger was like a cloth

everyone wore in that town, music was
not an item that could be confiscated,

removed by the fascists or the nuns
or the wealthy families that always

seem to be on the right side. This night
seven days before she will speak again

the road she must be walking inside
her sleep is smooth and inclines easily

into the mountains with a view over the sea.
Nothing about her within this dark room

indicates I'm there with her standing
on an edge confused by wind and her

presence or that I have ever been
born or that she's learned to speak

my language and I hers. Tonight
neither can decipher the other's tongue.

Our ancestry accounts for us—
some border crossing custom's

office floor is littered with pages
of our unpronounceable names.

THE REAL CAUSE FOR YOUR ABSENCE

In the afternoon the river thawed
and not one ice plate remained—
you could sit on the bank and watch
the flow float seed pods and tampon
boxes out of town, as if it were
a road you could stand beside
with your thumb out. Or skip a stone
from a pile the strange neighbor
boy mounded at your feet again.

This year, when the milk cartons
bobbed and twirled on the current,
the grocer seemed a little smaller
and our child gave her pocket stones
back to the riverbed. Suddenly tired,
the greasy mechanic had to look away
from the weasel dipping in and out
of the oak leaves lilting and twirling
in a mid-stream pool. Like last year,

like every year, the days were still
short and dropped their thick dark
hard like a wool quilt over the water.
The whole town went likewise to bed.
Not one lamp burned, which could have
given us a reason to stay. For a while
our bed felt perfect—firm, warm,
occupied—until the water drew our noise
from the windows and we followed—

You went upstream. I climbed down.

A HISTORY OF OAK TREES

These oaks held boys
once in their branches,
reaching their slender
limbs for leaf buds, shoes,
boxes of lemon drops, all
the things that boys stick
in bough crooks. They would
ride the tree limbs, giggle
and shake silent like sparrow
flutter when someone passed.

For hours one day their mothers
called, as if calling boys home
were their occupation. The boys
stayed. They had practiced sitting
still and had mastered becoming
part of the tree, that shivering
and whispering part on nights
like this when a woman sags
with her heavy bags and walks
alone beneath the branches
and into the dark these
street lights cannot reach.

AVIARY

Whole kernels of grain steam
in piles.

When dung darkens into dirt
beneath the stalks

cows glean, the farmer will herd them
to a new field.

My brothers work the acres in shifts,
dipping and raising, scooping

up muck-covered bean and corn kernels
then fly, digesting over acres,

like I used to nip at the souls
lingering above bodies

carried north in the morning
and south at dusk.

STILL LIFE WITH A BED IN THE MIDDLE

While I sleep my wife writes on my back.

She sits on top of me naked.
She wants me to feel what she writes.

When I wake the letter Q boils between my shoulder blades.

I think she traced K but there's longing in her
and she hates kites, kittens, even Kit Kat bars.

Her delicate hands hold desire, but fail
to translate it into the languages I understand.

She can juggle oranges, apples and pears.

She says the bed isn't large enough for what
this love traces from her finger tips.

The room diminishes when she opens her eyes.

LOOKING AT 12 WHITE THINGS

I forget to count the ticket stub
in my back pocket. A paperclip.
An envelope folded twelve times
to fit on the 4th row. A space
between the 2nd and 4th. Space is
a thing—the thingness, the gap
it creates. What lay beyond
the space, but a button I can't fit
to a shirt (attached to a notch
of fabric from the shirt I wore
yesterday). The hand that ripped it
off was white, too, but it won't stay
stuck to the paper sheet. I write
white hand and the letters form
the word that becomes the thing.
And while I'm cheating color,
lamp, though it's on the red table.
I write *edge of letter* though
the rest is coffee stained, and covered
with books. I have no white books,
so I write *no white book* and try
to get away with it. I own
an ink rag that's slowly turning blue.
A used stamp I've pealed off
an envelope. There's the dull sheen
on a needle threaded with red string.
If only I could put that sheen in there.
And the noise we call white, how
to put that on the page so when you
look at it, you don't hear me drowned out.

STILL LIFE WITH A MAN FALLING THROUGH IT

She'd never seen a tipping ladder or watched a man's foot
twenty rungs up press its weight on the step that wasn't there.

But the crows had seen worse mistakes and waited for another—
every bird knows a man's feet should never leave the earth,

a man was not meant to fly or float above the ground. It's a matter
of time, and the physics of shifting and slipping obey specific laws,

laws that require that a foot displaces space where there was no foot,
fills empty air, the ladder moves, falls and the man dies as the crows
       settle back to the branches above.

These words will be brush strokes, random dabs, then an arched line,
and now a breeze, light, leaves blinking on a tree. The tree is dead,

but the crows perch there above the woman in the house who is moving
out. She likes crows and thinks trees are what good people become

when they die and should never be cut down. She loves the tree
she thought died like her husband the day he was on a ladder

painting fascia boards and crows were flying past him to the elm
in the back yard. They filled each branch from bottom to top until

the tree was filled with a constant cawing that became a breathing-in-and-out,
like an asthmatic, at dusk. The man and woman were outside, one

on the ladder, the other in a chair keeping him company, *to keep him
from falling*, she thought, as if her presence might become a hand

that, if he slipped or misstepped, would hold him. She didn't hear the crows
caw or see any shit as they rose, as they scalded the leaves with their leaving.

She thinks the sky grew dark above the house because of their wings. She watched her husband slip, tilt, plunge to the ground in front of her chair,

as if she were the audience of a stunt requiring a man to cling to what was not there and climb inversely a ladder as it fell succinctly on top of him.

POSTCARD

Foreign, in this country,
my compass still spinning.
It can't find North, and every
cup and glass I drink is three
times higher than the pennies
the regulars pay. But I have
more here than back home.
I know how to get off this track.
No more wandering, no searching
for a fresh path leading to another
waterfall. I've seen enough
of those already. The tone
of my days comes out this way:
it appears in the floating calm
of a beach, on the tide, soft as rot
hanging in the air behind a bakery,
unable to climb against the wind
pushing down the mountainside.

A PLACE LIKE THIS

The red-wing blackbirds fight their fights
from the phone lines

above the foxtail wind-whipped in the ditch
below. Dust. Dust

everywhere after passing traffic and gravel pings
and pops crack open

afternoon silence this summer in the middle
of the country.

Don't ask about the turnips. Or what becomes of land
when what grows in far corners

isn't planted, is an end, a falling under like dusk, star glint,
day's heat sinking beneath the hills.

THE FALL

That day fixing the water tank, my half brother couldn't bear
what his father said, couldn't ingest the shove that was inside it,

and spun like one of the dogs that finally bristled at a shout or kick,
whined and simmered and growled at its whipped knees.

He became steadfast when his father turned
and pushed his back as he had before.

What must have gone through that man's mind
when his force met a greater one,

stopped, absorbed into that coiled spring his son had become
and jolted back?

There must have been a law, a prophecy at work:
the father pushes and pounds

the son for sixteen years, and in the seventeenth, the son pushes back
with greater force

the father who pushes back with greater force
the son

who now knows this time
he won't turn off the faucet

of muscle waiting in his chest, the swelling of years won't thrust his fist
to the barn door but back at his father

who has forgotten this day has been coming,
realizes his loss before losing it,

when the shock of the spring of his son's fist batters his breast.
This is how they both will fall

the moments the father is declining to the ground
budge eon-slow, like a massive river draws a barge down,

deliberate, unhindered
a hand where it shouldn't be, then the hot, spring afternoon

reveals cattle standing in the feedlot behind them, and chimney swallows
glittering in and out of the broken barn windows, sparrows gleaning the corn

dribbled from the bin, and regret is waiting
in the sharp pain that will glance up

when the man comes hard down on the ground.
That sudden

the landscape has been filled with the sound of a father tumbled
over gravel. Don't be confused,

there was no woman whispering to this son any word sounding like *knowledge*
or *innocence*. She offered nothing, not even a rotting apple.

This is a different story. Neither salvation nor sin
have a place here.

One man walks away while the other one
sits on stones stunned, shattered, and disobeyed.

FOLLOWING INSTRUCTIONS

I sat on the front steps watching
the chimney swifts fly over
the abandoned school like you
told me I should. They were paint
splatters across dusk. Before dark
crept out of the cracked windows

I made out trails of blue and purple
and followed the light shining

through their tails, but I got lost
in the buckeye tree's reaching leaf
rustle above the whipped grass,
and I could not decipher the pattern
weaving through the cracked glass.
I lost you somewhere in the failing
light, somewhere in the building's ruin.

I OPEN A BEER, A CAR APPROACHES

and I'm falling in love again. Today
with the air conditioner
as it shreds a nest of sparrows
and breathes a mist of down
into the room. I spent all morning
thinking I should tell my wife
about the pages I read yesterday
that make me want to sell each blue
shirt I own. The full moon
is a cliché, a festered wound
on the horizon, a helicopter
that distracts the stars rising
above the parkway traffic. . . .

A screen door hisses shut, and
outside this window the cedar,
pecan and that other tree bend
in air I can't feel. A knock,
then another at the neighbor's door.
The girls on bikes coast past a boy
weeping, *I don't want a haircut.*
I like my hair, as his father punches a doll.

TWO

As for those who face their death by wind
and call it by the weird name of forgiveness
they alone have the right to marry birds,
and those who stopped themselves from falling down
by holding the wall up or the sink in place
they can go without much shame for they
have lived enough and they can go click, click
if they want to, they can go tok, tok
and they can marry anything, even hummingbirds.

—GERALD STERN

SIX THIS MORNING

and I'm preoccupied with the price
of one of the angry little sparrows
outside, how much it would cost
to make, not to carve out of soap,
or whittle from balsa, but meld
flesh, blood, feathers,
down to the sharp, forked feet tips.

One January morning when ice
covered the trees, I blew one
to smithereens, as they say,
with a twenty-gauge shotgun,
but invisible was more like it—
not a fleck of blood or plume
remained speckled or scudding
across the snow or frozen to the pine.

I think about a night now as the sun
comes around, when I told a woman
how much I loved the reflection of light
on her skin, the wilting in her voice,
how she made me feel like I was ice,
her touch was heat that tempered me, these
words a trick, a lure to undress her
before my hands, then tongue
broke a thread between us, leaving little
trace of damage.

I drove home.

I broke that woman's heart.

How much for that?

RANT

I wake and say *Grackle*
to feel the metal of its gutturals
as if a car fender were falling,
giddy, madly in love with the tricycle
platform. Though I like more
the gust of air heaving

up the road of my throat and how
it crumbles the gravel there
into a song that gushes and jousts
with what would be music
had the scrawny canary not filled
its pea-size lungs instead. Give

me greasy head feathers, give me
broken-exhaust-pipe-clatter-
down-the-street-at-5am chirps
over the warbler song and the dove
coo and that swallow whistle
any day, and let me go back to sleep.

COLONY COLLAPSE DISORDER

The neighbors have a zucchini patch, but they are city folk and forgot
to plant the seeds together.

One plant flowered and the other didn't.

After two years I've forgotten the smell of my father's collar
when we embrace, his morning voice thrum as the coffee brews
and he reads the paper and waits for me to wake. No, to forget

would mean knowing and they didn't know what to plant or look for
to begin with. They saw one yellow fist of flower bloomed,

considered the beauty of yellow and how nature can be ugly, too and leave
another plant sterile half a yard away.

Half a country away this man is wilting in a house I haven't seen. To say
I didn't know what to look for would be as close to a lie as I could stand,

or that I forgot

proximity. Or that a home blooms because of the people who enter it.

Once I woke to his face staring at mine. I wish I had been four and thought
every father did this, but I was an exhausted twenty-seven, losing a wife

and sleeping off the morning maintenance shift on his couch.
We didn't speak; I closed my eyes and his pencil pulled
the lines and shade of my face onto a page.

Maybe the cause is as simple as fewer bees this year. Or too many
phone waves confuse them and they can't find their hive and fly
in endless turns. The dahlias, mums and petunias are exhausted bloomers.

Like a horse

ridden so hard for home it gets you there but its wind is broken, which means
its breath can't fill its lungs, even walking to the water tank exhausts it;

it's alive,

but there is no beauty there
but the beauty of the dying.

I have read what to do when flowers cannot be natural and don't bloom
on one side of a yard, but I don't know where to find how
a son should learn to care for his father. When.

My father's wife calls on Saturdays and describes the white petals
that have opened over his eyes. And, as if someone had put up a fence
across the yard of his brain, the words he says that once were clear and crisp

as January frost on glass are not ones he means—they are blocked, bent,
refracted light falling through.

Dialects disappear.

Your finger must become the bee, wander into that sticky womb
the petals make, linger there, poke, touch, wriggle, but be gentle,

like a nod to a lover in a crowded room to join you outside, in a closet
down the hall, or some benign place that becomes forbidden
when you are two. Dialing a phone is never enough.

Distance is an ugly relative and shouldn't decide why one goes home,
or when. I can't see a thing in the darkness

of the receiver's space when this man's voice tells me about paint, light,
the lines of a woman's face, how

he once wanted to touch a cheek Caravaggio seemed to create
like God created Eve's, kiss
the layers of paint on panel, but his was a whisper in a vast gap between us;

it's tight in the space his voice creates, Caravaggio removed, and I don't know
how to wiggle my way in to make a change.

As soon as I enter that realm one shouldn't fill I know there's a consequence—
for every action there is an opposite action: you enter your lover,
breath comes out,

a prickle of dust trickles from your finger and paints the delicate bud
asleep inside the flower skin.

I wait. Better to act like a bee and not think about the work my hands do,
haven't done, but keep moving, looking for flowers, for the soft heart of color

stuck inside pollen or whatever miracle of dust expanding to life
and look for that body my hands can mend.

RECITAL

She reads in a voice, my God, that voice
undresses me. Her pale skin seeps slowly
through the deep red gown. Who wouldn't
want to be alone with her in this crowded
room? I want to learn another language
for her, follow her to Poland and wait
for her to recognize me. I'm willing to quit
my job and leave my wife tonight. The back
yard smells heavy with sweet grapes and clipped
grass. Hell's door must be around here somewhere.

READING RICHARD HUGO TO MY NIECE

She asks for a funny one this time, so I read "Shark Island" and try
to give a different life to Hugo's poem.

She sits facing me and tracing the bridge of her nose—
she sucks her thumb and looks out the window in this house
where her mother and I fought, hid, but did not laugh like

she does now in front of me when I shout *We lean back under a sky
wide as spread arms, sparkling with scales.* She laughs for us.

She cleans out the silence with her little giggle, understanding Hugo's
humor, or maybe it's his gloom she finds humorous.

Little girl with so much waiting to damper out your smile, laugh
now. Laugh

at the world so I can join you.

But it's here in my reading
that she touches my leg with her other hand, pets me as if I

were the dog her grandmother keeps locked in a cage in the room beneath us.
The poem ends and she whispers, *Let's go and wake
Idoia*, though Idoia's awake

in a bed at the end of the hall. We walk, and in little shouts

we find ourselves standing, looking at this woman's body.

I tell her to kiss the sleeping cheek. She doesn't, but folds her hands

instead and looks at me, which means *You do it*, so I do. I turn back
and this little thing of love, this life balanced on two legs holds
every possible laughter in the world. *Now you*, I tell her.

She looks and must see the same beauty I do and doesn't know if she can
touch it, how or if she'll break it and get in trouble. Her hands touch the bed

and trace a line on the sheet, she looks up at me and says, *I just did*
and her lie is a truth we share, this skill of kissing
in our minds those we want but our hands can't bear to let us hold.

WALKING AROUND

Like all men who were boys and grew into pants
their mothers bought long, boys whose legs stretched

over the dark bed edge under heavy quilts pressing
air from their heaving lungs, I forget to turn on the heat

until I see my breath. I like to watch my coffee steam,
imagine those wisps bending behind the air in front of me

as if there were some transparent pocket they fold inside.

The sounds of a morning house—spoon din in the coffee
can, cup clank on the saucer—are crisper, cleaner when

degrees drop and hover over frost chill. The sky's dirty
white, a heavy mist, almost sleet, almost snow, hangs in

front of everything out there, waiting to clothe the cars
and early walkers. On days like this I walk with my hands

in my pockets. I've been told that's the wrong way to walk
but walking makes me think I've learned to do something

right, a skill mastered after years of practice,
and learned this lesson: to stomp my feet, toss my arms

around my shoulders to *Thwunk Thwunk* the blood flowing.

This chorus of slaps beneath wet cottonwood and oak, shed doors
latched shut, is a translation of a song a whip sings as it bites a calf.

DRAWING OF A BOY FORGETTING

Before the uncertain streets,
    before buildings high and glittery, fruit
    vendors selling long pieces of yellow,

        before the lines waiting, joining lines,
        endless water spreading, the heaving
        waves, vomit, the tight wool suit
        inherited from the neighbor killed
        by a bull's hoof to the head,
        the photograph's luxurious sheen
        behind glass on the mantle behind
        the neighbors wringing their hands
        and staying back, their compressed
        breath, tear-stained hugs,

            before steamer trunk scuttle, packing
            in the kitchen, the last dawn and smell
            of old leather polished new, creaking
            like floors in a foreign house,

                before a woman had to make the decision
                to leave because no man lived to make it,
                the boy remembers watching his brother
                crawl into the lilac bush shadow—
                white lace embroidered with dirt
                perfume and pale purple buds
                tumbled on the ground.

                Before the war's end they would leave
                their family tree withered, lug trunks,
                bags, a box filled with cloth, a cross,
                thread, pins, needles, a jar of burial dirt
                for the photographs of the dead left behind.

The boy forgot his family, his friends,
the shine in the shoes on his feet
when he saw the ship dockside.

>He walked on water,
>and he was dumb with watching
>the sun outline his arm and hand
>on the deck as countrysides,
>hills and valleys of ocean crumbled,
>divided for the hull, as the deep
>surrounded the land, until there
>were no more gulls, until blue,
>black and white were endless, until
>the wind sounded like air under gull
>feathers and there were gulls with wind
>under their feathers again, a thread
>line of darkness on the distance, then
>an arm, a crowned statue, an island
>of crowds, faces in a maze of gazes
>and halls, high windows and echoes, bold
>men uniformed in blue, their fingers
>wrapped fat around pencils, pressing
>pages of names and numbers flat, others
>pushing, shouting, herding and writing
>in chalk on each back: *Passage*, or
>*Pinkeye*, or *Socialist*, or *Criminal*, *Return*,
>gleaning the grain for the future
>of a world across the water.

>>The boy could not read to his brother
>>the familiar letters in foreign orders,
>>the sign above the exit. He walked
>>forward. He crossed the threshold.

LUNCH WITH THE KIWANIS CLUB

A man enters a room full of men, two
women, the town's business people
standing after a bell rings to pledge,
sing, then listen while the club president
recites a prayer. Their heads bow
and the man hears words like *father*,
trespass, *kingdom* and *forever*, sees
them sit and eat in silence what
they eat in this country, and after
sees them bend deeper in their chairs
as their guest, an unknown son of
the town who left and has returned
wearing the color of difference, stands,
ducks and nods to discuss living
beyond their county's borders. He reads
three poems and no questions follow.
Applause is an obligation the crowd fulfills
before shuffling away, and the last man
in the room nods, his face puffy with years
behind a desk, his shoulders like fields
curling over a hill while his hand takes
the poet's, holds it like he does a child's,
or dog's paw, or some object he doesn't understand.
What follows is a calm that elapses
like seed germination, like quiet around cattle
grazing through high grass, the end of a summer
work-day twenty years before in hay fields
when tractor engines and machines click cool
and a slight nod from a neighbor who hired him
means go home but come back tomorrow,
which means he is worth paying, he knows
what work is and his work is good.

WHITEOUT

There's a Russian word for getting lost
in the snow, and like everything Russian
there's more to it than getting turned around
on your way to the store for bread or matches.

You are suddenly in a life, not knowing which
way your face is facing in the white before you.
You are falling, and which way becomes a puzzle
you've put together a thousand times but now

don't know how to frame. You think your feet
are beneath you, your head on your shoulders,
and the sky above. But you are wrong. The word
includes this confusion. In this whiteout today

the trees wedge me in. Soon they'll be gone—
the sidewalk a track, then a river, then the guiling
snow will drift it into the road until the neighborhood
becomes a blur, a photo of a place I remember

from my grandfather's lap, that man telling me
about the coldest winter he endured, but his horse
did not, frozen in the middle of the pasture, its eyes
suddenly glass at some moment in the storm,

and when dawn came, they were the first to melt,
as if staring at the sun could do that to eyes.

The snow on the roof melted, though the horse
still stood, looking east, a hind leg bent the way
they do, and the others still firm on the ground.
My grandfather thought the horse was strong,

sturdy—to have weathered the ice and blowing—
when he looked up from his chores and saw it

there in the growing light. But like a clack
and crunch out here pulls your eyes to watch

a tree limb's slow and definite break and fall,
or a visitor driving down the lane with news,
a crack began and soon the horse was shivering
the ice and powder from its back, the way

they flounce the flies in summer off a specific spot.
A cloud rose up around it, a kind of storm itself,
and any life inside that standing carcass was spent
in falling down in the crash it carried over the frozen

clods below its hooves. My grandfather liked to tell me,
sitting there with him inside on cold white days,
completely white outside, it forgot what standing
meant, and sometimes when you forget, you fall.

THREE

Wine tells the truth. Now I am wine.

Wine is the sun.

Wine, the sun and you, three things worth dying for.

—JORGE GIMENO

HOME

My hands and back flinch. It's god
damn depressing and empty, the Iowa
farm—flying over those hills rolling,
every inch infested with more white
houses, imploding barn and stock yards—
this place I come from. It's so dismal
in its vacancies of neighbors waving
and talking I can't remember
happiness there some days in such dust
and living in stench with cattle, hogs
and corn, and wanting to stay.
                                           Someone
must have found it beautiful: the grand-
fathers and mothers now blind in low
brick nursing homes smelling of ammonia,
sweat and feed—they are children wetting
their beds again, dreaming of the earth
plot that will pay back their work. The town
drunk in Williamsburg lived in a shed
on the print shop parking lot. He must have
looked out the floppy door in the morning
and watched the sun rise over the dogwood,
like I did once. All of them will be gone
before I get to the end of this and the plane
lands in another state, and I won't see my mother
again until I must, which will be the last time.

THREE SPAIN SKETCHES

This makes a city: the Grand Via
bum with no legs asleep on the bus.

Malasaña hipsters wearing heavy
shoes and eyeing a woman
in a white parka on the platform
watching her reflection blink
in the passing train windows.

I'd like to slip somehow
beneath those repetitious
clackings and get inside
her skin, wear her
bones and sense her center's
thump, her growing breath
and body forced forward.

Another part of this landscape
holds an image of the street's
rising and falling tones, and follows
the sound seeping from it,
the city's voice and base
color falling into a speck
on the horizon in the setting
turn of day when shadows
grow in a central plaza
as the tram passes through it.

~

A mountain alone at night
east of here, east of these
windows, where beech
trees endure the dark
like waiting for a curse,
a threat to unfold. Someone
clacks castanets. There
is a clamoring. I've seen
something like that
outside a bus window
in Madrid. I was the only one
awake watching the city
come to first light
on the M-30, and the bus
seemed to float from north
to south, and junkies on a train
switch box, sitting like children
would on a summer day watching
the morning traffic grow, dangling
their feet down, their shoes thumped
on the cold metal beneath them, each
breath a wisp of white in front of them.

~

I don't hear any music today
but as I walk I clack
softly. I've grown into my shoes
but my shirt billows bigger,
doubles my size when I face the wind.
I don't know how to draw
an image off the landscape and float
it into the air around my ears,
under my feet as if…as if muscle might
possess the life these sketches
embody. A train starts, so gradual
we don't know if the wagon is moving
or the people on the platform
have said goodbye and started to walk away.

LETTER FROM ANOTHER COUNTRY

I need air moving through the house, moving
around me—Did I tell you our windows,
all except one, are painted shut? I'm working,

but I'm looking out one now
because last night I thought my eyes
had slid from my head; I'm sweating in this

back room just thinking about it. I feel like
taking a walk, or at least standing outside, but
it's muggy and the mosquitoes.... The trees

here hold their green then turn orange
for a moment, like that moment
I was weaving through that city

with a number instead of a name in central Russia
before the wall came down and I looked up
as if I wanted to see the blue sky I used to stare at

on a farm on the other side of the world, the one
I knew you were under, but instead I saw
the bare sagging breasts of a woman looking out

her apartment window, a cigarette dangling from her mouth,
tipping ash on her brown nipple as she shifted to watch
the traffic below, or the leaves, or the fly dying on her sill.

She was above me looking down like the leaves here
must miss their life so much they can no longer bear
the sight of themselves on these branches

and all they have to hold is their green. I'm afraid
winter will be sudden, that I won't see the leaves
turn or their falling, only what's left on the ground.

JACARANDA LOVE SONG

In May the jacaranda blooms
the color of my eyes. Across the street
they heaved with flowers when I arrived
and their branches sagged and my eyes wept.
The air fills with sweet pollen that bathes
everything in yellow most afternoons,
from bare-shouldered barmaids to the tourists'
walking shoes. It is dangerous to breathe here,
and my lungs are hungry for a different color,
one closer to the yellow earth on the city outskirts.
It's hot, but there's always the shaded side
of the street and after rain our breath
is heavy, green, and the jacaranda is the tree
these people peel for their flamenco guitars.
I praise the dominance of the passive voice
and the man who couldn't bare the silence
of blooming wood and bent a limb
and hacked a trunk to turn timber into fluttering,
whispered sorrow. The wood, once it is cut
and knows it can no longer push out flowers
and perfume, wails and moans its loss,
and the guitarist, that man in the corner
room above the park, the one who understands
gut and grain, can make notes that float above us
clinging to the space between the dark branches.

SKETCHBOOK SONNET #38—ON CLOUDS

Today clouds walk through this mountain town. Some slow,
hardly leaning, climbing—they are a crowd of laughing women
chattering as they amble a paved path through the trees. Others,
wisps of fast, thin light lurch and swerve lean and aloof.
They will disappear if I look away. So I do not look away

but pull at their circles and bulges and hips as if they were
a woman's. I can't draw anything on the page the way I see it—
tenderness, their annoyance, ridicule, laughter. I keep looking,
like a voyeur watching new lovers in a field, yes, like watching
them linger and tremble. I'm lost. The view slips. These lines

have become figures in my hands, and I let them touch me.
Clouds gather, where the mountain beech, pine, and oak
breathe, like rocks trickled over with moss my fingers traced
after making love once on pine needles. The same white air
sifted over the sea then, embossed the branches above
and ignored me beneath, its vapors rippled, not waiting.

BEGINNING WITH A EUCALYPTUS LEAF

A friend has sent me Greece by post.
She began with a leaf

slender, green and pungent as if
dried on a terrace beside the sea.

Next she sent a pebble,
one peeled from the wall of her room.

She carried it with her to the beach, washed
it in the sea. I can taste the salt water.

Weeks without a letter and today
a thin envelope in the mailbox.

Her hand has scrawled this note
in place of the return address:

*Open this letter in a hushed room when
you remember you still haven't opened it.*

I understand her. The envelope
was filled with the sound

of the night in Naxos—a late traveler dropping
his bag, or a crab pulling itself onto a rock.

The last letter she wrote never arrived. The postman
said it was too big to deliver and gave me

a wrinkled yellow receipt that smells of rosemary
and scratches my hands when I touch it.

My skin tans when I hold it. I keep it
in my desk and open the drawer when I need heat.

SKETCHBOOK SONNETS #53 & #54—A DUST SPECK THAT USED TO BE A MAN

The crows call your name from the high branches
as if they could read your thoughts as you sit here
in the shade looking up at them looking down at you
looking up at them perched in trees I don't know
how to name. You distract them. Their brothers
gather over on Elm Street above Mercy Hospital—
someone's dead. A few flakes of snow, so few
I'm certain I could count them and start but then
forget when I hear your steps. One crow barks
like a puppy, another above me, the one treading air,
croaks. The councils on small murders gather.

~

I am sitting in *la Plaza de Gracia* with a man
who could be Shahid but says he's Italian
and we're listening to pigeons shuffle and coo.
He smells like orange blossoms, and his voice
is the sound of hoof scuffs on stones in the *albaicin*.
He tells a story about spice in the courtyard of lions,
then laughs. His hands remind me of a gypsy girl
dancing for coins. When I tell him this he says
they will buy our memories with *centimos* they beg
from tourists. He tells me the pack burros climbing
these streets are cursed to carry the lost notes
of Lorca's last song. He says the swallows circling
stopped trying to pluck them out long ago.

SOUTH OVERTON

I speak this neighborhood's name
to the nicked brick and cobble,
to the yard on 15th overgrown
with morning glory and jimson
we used to call weeds because
they'd do to a combine what some
food will do to a body—bind up
the workings of the machine.
But I'm not back North in Iowa,
on a Williamsburg street dead-ending
at the edge of town where the cold
has pushed color into oak, maple
and catalpa leaves; I'm down here
at South Overton, South. Over. Ton.
Southoverton. And I see two boys
and ask, *¿Donde está la frontera
de Sobre tonelada del Sur?*
They ride away and I yell, *O se dice
'South Overton aquí?* Sometimes
I find myself at intersections, at places
where traffic circles or waits and I wait, too,
for the passing. The passing air
mostly, because there's nothing
else moving over here today so I walk
south over town, over the street. No,
I'm riding my bike and I'm stopped
at the traffic circle on W and 15th
watching the confusion at the intersection
and that's a word I'd like to hold
in my mouth a while as I stand
outside the doors of the Pioneer Land
& Cattle Company shifting my weight
on the empty stoop, glancing at the mail
stuffed box, the fliers tossed
down the steps and now over my shoulder

to the woman in shorts and a sweater walking
with a dog. There's no leash between them.
The dog follows her, stops when she stops
to tie her shoe, like two friends walking
together, and I miss my friends, the weather,
and where'd the time go because
down the street the Center Point apartments
are fighting and having dinner, like last night
and the night before, and a low-rider waits
for me to get on my bike and pedal, ride by,
everyone inside watching me balance
my cigarette, pedal and push up my glasses.
I want to ride by the woman
getting in her car again…sweet perfume,
from her eyes and smile, but Jaime and Carlos
are singing and pedaling their sisters' bikes
on my left, riding through puddles, singing,
Oh my God. Oh my God, for the jagged
music splashing with them through the water.
15th street is okay, but I don't like the letter F,
its sound, but 16th will do, and not only does S
remind me of supper, but this block farther in
from Q has houses with more than dirt
for lawns or patches of weeds, and at T
the houses start to blush in the late afternoon,
as if life were coming to the windows,
doors and awnings to watch this white guy
on a bike and not in a car, or the fall in the air
under the shade tree, the leaf scuttle
along the street, following those boys on bikes.

SKETCHBOOK SONNET #86—A NORTHERN PROVINCE

The river crawls through the rain this morning,
an untended fence standing before me.
Last year I didn't see its form when I
sketched that rock between the patio door
and river, shaded in its top and sides,
smooth and ice-covered beside snow-covered
grass. The river swells every day inside
itself, hides its currents and suspends its
pools, attempts to erase its banks. There is
no failure in this water rubbing out
the bank lines, and no bottom, no place in
it which is not river. The north bank is
closer than yesterday, deeper,
the water sifting through another day.

WHILE HYDRANGEAS ARE FALLING

the bull enters through the fanfare and there's the matador twirling his cape, and those banderilleros with their flashy pants and batons—barbed on the end—can't wait to stab and dash, and the picador on his well-wrapped beast beneath him jousts the bull, then waits for the breathing horns and tendons, the muscle-thick mass to get bored and move away. This is about lessons, an education. In this school, the matador is the lucid professor, shedding light on the student's monochromatic vision of the world to draw him into the ring. He teaches the bull to hate the elusive cape, teaches us to follow what moves, to fix our attention on the bull's horn tips until his fist and wrist and voice shivers into the fabric and the bull's muscles flex and explode forward. We are learning to look for beauty in the damaged bull's hump. The bull is learning to love the cape. But the bull is slow, a troubled student. He needs long moments to reflect, to realize that peculiar, uncomfortable smell in the air is blood, his own bleeding, and he spends the rest of the lesson looking in the cape for what he's losing. In these last moments we learn *this* is art. This is culture. A good kill.

VALLE DE ATXONDO

Christmas and I am in
the mountains with a man

whose second language
is like smoke on the valley

walls. We turn on our path
where a farmer spades

freezing muck beside
his sputtering tractor. Our

dialects clod in that earth
pile and this chimney

of a man beside me
dissipates. He had nothing

in his hands to drop,
to announce his disappearance.

My shirt smells like fire.

WHILE READING I THINK ABOUT DRAWING

Flowers grow inside my wife—

red, pink, white petunias, poppies and lilacs—the petals
dry on the stems of her ribs.

Every morning is a new year here.

I'm waiting for the jittery red and blue birds I have never seen
before tonight to fall asleep.

My grandfather used to say, *If swallows rest before
midnight the stars will shine until dawn*, but

that's not written in any books.

The landscape of Atxondo is like a memory of lost birds and fitful sleep,
and waiting wide awake for the first glimmers of a red dawn.

Listen

to the chimney swifts.
They don't know how to be dishonest.

Or to the dogs playing with water.

These mountains make me a new man.

I still learn from the cherry trees, the barbed wire
stretching up the hill, and the grass blades lapping

on a rock, and that space between each blade.

EL EJIDO

They kick a flat rubber ball, the neighborhood kids,
up and down the street—their game will decide how
they will eat their dinner, but not when their fathers
will leave the bar. Tomorrow they become new boys
running to a fight and the day after, men who gather
near the post office to smoke and escape rooms
where they are silenced by their wives or the radio.

The police wear masks in the plaza as they gather
to guard the port. Yesterday one dropped his baton
on the shoulders of a man with coins in his pockets
and dirt in his cuffs. The bone cracking sounded
like twigs he snapped over his knee when he was six.

In another province, on the morning after a bomb
exploded and the man who carried it stopped
being a man and became blood on shards of glass,
women leaned out empty frames where the day
before they had opened their windows. They
shook dust from their rugs and mops and wind
rose from the street and carried it away.

SAETAS

I ask my friend whose mother died
from a hole that wouldn't stop growing
in her stomach, and whose aunt is dying
from holes consuming her mouth,
if he's ever heard a *saeta* when
he tells me that on Mother's Day
he and his two brothers sang karaoke
in Chinatown, brothers who have sweet
voices that can lull screaming children
to sleep, brothers who have bloodied
their knuckles for fun and beaten
men like me unconscious because
they wanted to, I tell him I first heard
the saeta on a street in Cordoba
the year I fell out of love,
that the woman singing beside me
closed her eyes and sang in a voice
more immense than the buildings
around us, *Guapa, es la flor que enciende
el dia. Perdoneme. Perdone a los mios.*
He tells me the dying women he knows
pray his belly is filled, that his face
shouldn't worry. He reminds me
that even the faithless pray. My prayers
come as I'm watching and listening
to the music in this city, which could be
any city where women turn my head,
men have stumps for legs, a stench of piss
and shit on asphalt lingers under more music
spilling out of open windows…a broken dish,
a hand slapping a face, a door squeaking open
and closed in the wind, or that which fills
rooms with silence as I sit with a friend
waiting for words, songs, even prayers
to come to his lips in the dark of another country.

LILAC IN SEVILLA

Believe I haven't left my wife,
that my hands are now leaves,

my arms branches and my hair
and fingernails flowering

buds. Believe this woman
has kept me quenched

and has fed me. Where calluses
curled my palms into fists

smooth branches twine their way up,
sun curious, wind and rain curious.

I dream of stretching,
and at night I stretch into black

sky above me. The earth my feet burrow.
Her hair makes a sound

I imitate when I shiver.
Her hands trace my leaves.

She breathes.
I can touch her lungs.

DRAWINGS

I might as well begin with a bucket and a well or a deep
hole, so deep dark is a reflection of midnight, the world

the other way around, the dark in a cave core
we don't have a definition or word that fits. I will

name it for you and draw from anguish, from rot and rut, from
Polar South, from zocolo, from rectum, from niche,

from crevasse, from Juarez, Darfur and El Ejido,
race and rope, from under painting, back-handed swipe

at a cheek, chimney sweep face-stain, great depression
hunger and pogrom cold, from Guernica's severed arm

at the bottom of the painting, the black specks in the distance
dropping on the town my father-in-law watched from a mountain

top the day he and his family picnicked and the German planes
warmed up their guns on them and their sun-bleached cloth,

and the rocks they hid behind and the bombs falling and smoke
plumes above the town.

                    I draw from that smoke, their fear,
that child's curiosity, and the dark sounds he heard. And

Lorca's *duende* and my friend Sizzle's rage that led him
to love—there is darkness there between them—

and in Patricio's neck buckled under faith, knees
kneeling on rice, the shade between his skin and those kernels,

the bottom of Alexander's glass in a Philly street. I draw from
the grief that hides Sebastian. And Elaine's empty hands

she tries to fill by cupping water and pulling herself through
Long Island Sound, and the dark stain on Jeet's hands he can't wash

away since the night Shakti left her shadow on a floor somewhere in Delhi.
In the number 7 on this page, the letter Q, the place where it begins

and the war where it ends.
                              And fissure and incision and the blood

opaque water they leave when my wife weeps in the bathroom…
and what I don't know what to say to any of this and to the void

in a girl's head that feasts on years she should have lived.
     Like bombs

feast on air sucked from the lungs of mothers and children walking
home from church before drawing the rubble down on top of them.

Like holding the wide-eyed horse close, soothing its velvet nose
to close its eyes, embracing its neck and helping to draw a last breath.

NOTES

"You Know You Want It" is for James Hoch and Sebastian Matthews.
"Home" is after Robert Winner.
"Still Life With A Bed In The Middle" is for Idoia Elola.
"Reading Richard Hugo To My Niece" is for Cetera Plagmann.
"Lunch With The Kiwanis Club" is after Philip Levine.
"Whiteout" is for Jennifer Acker.
"Sketchbook Sonnets #53 & #54" is for Jeet Thayil.
"Beginning With A Eucalyptus Leaf" is for Elaine Sexton.
"Saetas" is for Patrick Rosal.
"Drawings" is dedicated to several people. They know who they are.

Curtis Bauer is the author of two poetry collections: his first, *Fence Line*, won the John Ciardi Poetry Prize, and *Spanish Sketchbook* is a bilingual English/Spanish collection published by Ediciones en Huida in Seville Spain. His poems and translations have appeared in *The Southern Review, The Indiana Review, The Common* and *The American Poetry Review*, among others. He is the publisher and editor of Q Avenue Press Chapbooks, the Spanish Translations Editor for *From the Fishouse*, and he teaches Creative Writing and Translation at Texas Tech University in Lubbock, Texas and Seville Spain.

CPSIA information can be obtained
at www.ICGtesting.com
Printed in the USA
LVHW101522161019
634412LV00006B/359/P